Global Biodiversity Assessment
Summary for Policy-Makers

R.T. Watson (Chair), V.H. Heywood (Executive Editor),
I. Baste, B. Dias, R. Gámez, T. Janetos, W. Reid, G. Ruark

UNEP

Published for the
United Nations Environment Programme

CAMBRIDGE
UNIVERSITY PRESS

The book *Global Biodiversity Assessment* is published by Cambridge University Press.
ISBN 0 521 56403 4 hardback   ISBN 0 521 56481 6 paperback

Co-ordinators of the Global Biodiversity Assessment
Professor Vernon H. Heywood and Mr Ivar Baste (*Section 1*)
Dr Frank A. Bisby (*Section 2*)
Professor David L. Hawksworth and Professor Mary T. Kalin-Arroyo (*Section 3*)
Professor Robert Barbault and Dr Setijati D. Sastrapradja (*Section 4*)
Professor Harold A. Mooney, Dr Jane Lubchenco, Dr Rodolfo Dirzo and Dr Osvaldo E. Sala
   (*Sections 5 and 6*)
Dr Nigel E. Stork and Professor Michael J. Samways (*Section 7*)
Professor David L. Hawksworth (*Section 8*)
Dr Silvio Olivieri, Mr Jerry Harrison and Dr John R. Busby (*Section 9*)
Dr Bryan A. Barlow and Dr George T. Tzotzos (*Section 10*)
Mr Jeffrey A. McNeely, Dr Madhav Gadgil, Professor Christian Levèque, Dr Christine Padoch and
   Dr Kent Redford (*Section 11*)
Professor Charles Perrings (*Section 12*)
Dr Kenton Miller, Dr Mary H. Allegretti, Mr Nels Johnson and Professor Bror Jonsson (*Section 13*)

ISBN 0 521 56480 8 paperback
GE

Contents

Foreword

Biodiversity represents the very foundation of human existence. Yet by our heedless actions we are eroding this biological capital at an alarming rate. Even today, despite the destruction that we have inflicted on the environment and its natural bounty, its resilience is taken for granted. But the more we learn of the workings of the natural world, the clearer it becomes that there is a limit to the disruption that environment can endure.

Besides the profound ethical and aesthetic implications, it is clear that the loss of biodiversity has serious economic and social costs. The genes, species, ecosystems and human knowledge that are being lost represent a living library of options available for adapting to local and global change. Biodiversity is part of our daily lives and livelihoods and constitutes the resources upon which families, communities, nations and future generations depend.

The basis of any discipline is not the answers it gets, but the questions it asks. As an exercise in biodiversity conservation, a number of questions can be asked: What are the values associated with biodiversity? How can benefits be generated from this resource? How can these benefits be shared in a fair and equitable manner? How do humans influence biodiversity? What are the underlying causes for this influence and what are their ecological consequences? How do the natural dynamics of biodiversity and the human-induced changes in biodiversity affect the values and goods and services provided by biodiversity to society?

Taken together, these questions bring out the multi-dimensional challenge that the issue of biodiversity conservation poses to policy-makers and scientists alike.

Fortunately, the international community has recognized this challenge. The entry into force of the Convention on Biological Diversity, in December 1993, is illustrative not only of this recognition but also of a change in the overall strategy in conserving biodiversity. It signals a move to a more proactive position that simultaneously seeks to meet people's needs from biological resources while ensuring the long-term sustainability of Earth's biological capital.

The United Nations Environment Programme has played a key role in the development of the issues relating to biodiversity. Our efforts have included the forging of the Convention on Biological Diversity its follow-up, and have included efforts to strengthen the national and global base of knowledge on biodiversity.

This endeavour lies at the very core of UNEP's three-fold mandate:

- to catalyse awareness on global environmental problems;
- to build consensus on action to address those problems;

- to promote and support successful programmes and activities of a catalytic nature.

An essential element is the collection and dissemination of knowledge generated by scientific research. In this regard the scientific community has been and shall continue to be UNEP's key partner in carrying out our mandate.

It was in this spirit that UNEP commissioned the Global Biodiversity Assessment (GBA) project. Underlying this endeavour was an attempt to mobilize the global scientific community to analyse the present state-of-the-art knowledge and understanding of biodiversity and the nature of our interactions with it: in other words, to provide the scientific information to answer some of the questions posed above.

It must be noted here that unlike the global agreements on Climate Change and Ozone Depletion, no formal scientific assessment was carried out prior to the final negotiation of the Convention on Biological Diversity. The Parties to the Convention clearly recognize the lack of knowledge regarding biodiversity, and the urgent need to develop our knowledge base in this area. However, let me hasten to add, there have been no formal links between the Assessment and the Convention.

Nevertheless, governments were regularly informed of the progress made in the development of this document. UNEP was gratified when we received written submissions from experts from more than 50 countries, who peer-reviewed various parts of the Assessment in their personal capacity.

The document produced is the result of an ambitious scientific endeavour, the outcome of the invaluable contributions of more than a thousand experts worldwide. It reflects a broad spectrum of views.

The GBA is an independent critical, peer-reviewed scientific analysis of the current issues, theories and views regarding the main aspects of biodiversity. The Assessment does not concern itself with the assessment of the state of country-level or regional biodiversity. This was the fear expressed by some constituencies when this project was initiated. Its perspective is global with a focus on general concepts and principles. It does not present any policy recommendations, although it does draw attention to possible policy implications of its major findings and to existing gaps in knowledge and capacity.

Although the GBA does provide an analysis of a wide range of biological and social science issues pertaining to biodiversity, its range is by no means exhaustive. Issues such as fair and equitable sharing of benefits, financial mechanisms and technology transfer have not been treated as extensively as the more scientific issues.

The emergence of new issues – scientific, economic and social – relating to biodiversity in the near future is a distinct possibility. In this context GBA should be regarded as a timely assessment of the subject as perceived by the global scientific community.

UNEP believes that the GBA will provide a compendium of knowledge for the benefit of those involved in the implementation of the Convention on Biological Diversity and it will also serve as a useful tool for the scientific body of the Convention to begin its work. I also hope that the Assessment will provide a significant conceptual input in the implementation of the relevant chapters of Agenda 21 and some initiatives put forth by the Commission on Sustainable Development (CSD).

Clearly the aim of the Assessment was not to present a consensus document. It is, however, an important step in building scientific consensus and creating the foundation for implementing political consensus. It is my fond hope that the GBA will succeed on both these counts. This Summary for Policy-Makers presents the main conclusions drawn by the Assessment, with an emphasis on those aspects that will be of interest to policy-makers.

Elizabeth Dowdeswell
Executive Director, UNEP

Editors' Preface

This Summary for Policy-Makers has been prepared by an editorial group, and is based largely on the information provided in the Executive Summaries of the different Sections that make up the Global Biodiversity Assessment (GBA). The contributions of the Section Co-ordinators of the GBA to this process constituted a major input and are gratefully acknowledged here. This Summary has been extensively peer-reviewed and an earlier draft was discussed at a GBA workshop held in Panama, 12–16 June 1995.

In preparing this Summary we have attempted to present the main conclusions that have been reached by the Assessment and particular emphasis has been placed on those that will be of most interest to policy-makers.

We are grateful to T. Lovejoy and P.H. Raven for their comments on earlier drafts which have helped add clarity to certain aspects of the Summary. Inès Verleye (UNEP) has assisted with the selection of illustrations and the World Conservation Monitoring Centre has also helped in providing figures.

R.T. Watson
V.H. Heywood
I. Baste
B. Dias
R. Gámez
A. Janetos
W. Reid
G. Ruark

Biodiversity is a vital resource for all humankind

The Earth is home to a rich and diverse array of living organisms, whose genetic diversity and relationships with each other and with their physical environment constitute our planet's biodiversity. *This biodiversity is the natural biological capital of the Earth, and presents important opportunities for all nations.* It provides goods and services essential to support human livelihoods and aspirations, and enables societies to adapt to changing needs and circumstances. The protection of these assets, and their continued exploration through science and technology, offer the only means by which the nations of the world can hope to develop sustainably. The ethical, aesthetic, spiritual, cultural and religious values of human societies are an integral part of this complex equation.

The limited knowledge base

The distribution and magnitude of the biodiversity that exists today is a product of over 3.5 billion years of evolution, involving speciation, migration, extinction, and, more recently, human influences. *Recent estimates of the total number of species range from 7 to 20 million, but we believe a good working estimate is between 13 and 14 million of which only about 1.75 million species have been scientifically described, just under a fifth of them plants or vertebrates.* Less well studied groups of organisms include bacteria, arthropods, fungi and nematodes, while species that live in marine environments and beneath the ground are especially poorly known.

Even for the 1.75 million species that have been described, there is no comprehensive listing and we have a highly incomplete and patchy understanding of their reproductive biology, their demography, the chemicals they contain, their ecological requirements and the roles they play in ecosystems. Genetic diversity within species is known well for only a very small number of species – primarily those that have direct importance for human health, scientific research and economic exploitation.

The threat to nature's adaptability

Diversity of species and genes affects the ability of ecological communities to resist or recover from disturbances and environmental change, including long-term climatic change. Genetic variation within species is the ultimate basis for evolution, the adaptation of wild populations to local environmental conditions, and the development of animal breeds and cultivated crop varieties which have yielded significant direct benefits to humanity. Losing the diversity of genes within species, species within ecosystems, and ecosystems within a region makes it ever more likely that further environmental disturbance will result in serious reductions in the goods and services that the Earth's ecosystems can provide.

Biodiversity is being destroyed by human activities at unprecedented rates

The adverse effects of human impacts on biodiversity are increasing dramatically and threatening the very foundation of sustainable development. The rate at which humans are altering the environment, the extent of those alterations, and their consequences for the distribution and abundance of species, ecological systems, and genetic variability are unprecedented in human history, and pose substantial threats to sustainable economic development and the quality of life. Loss of biological resources and their diversity threatens our food supplies, sources of wood, medicines and energy, opportunities for recreation and tourism, and interferes with essential ecological functions such as the regulation of water runoff, the control of soil erosion, the assimilation of wastes and purification of water, and the cycling of carbon and nutrients.

The downward spiral

During the last few millennia species have been made extinct as a result of human activities. Prehistoric colonization of islands in the Pacific and Indian oceans some 1000 to 2000 years ago by humans and their commensals, rats, dogs and pigs, may have led to the extinction of as many as a quarter of the world's bird species. Since 1600, 484 animal and 654 plant species are recorded as having gone extinct although this is almost certainly an underestimate, especially as regards tropical regions. *Based on an assumed average life span of 5 to 10 million years for organisms with adequate fossil records, the extinction rate for these groups has been estimated to be fifty to a hundred times the average expected natural rate.* In addition, there has been widespread loss of populations and genetic resources.

Because of the world-wide loss or conversion of habitats that has already taken place, tens of thousands of species are already committed to extinction. It is not possible to take preventive action to save all of them. Projections of impending extinctions due to habitat loss can be made using the empirical relationship between the number of species and the area of a habitat, derived from island biogeography. When applied to tropical forests, published estimates of the number of species that will eventually become extinct or committed to extinction due to projected forest loss over the next 25 years or so range from 2% to 25% in the various groups examined (mainly plants and birds): this would be equivalent to 1000 to 10 000 times the expected background rate. If recent rates of loss of closed tropical forest (about 1% globally per year) were to continue for the next 30 years, the equilibrium number of species in the forest, as calculated by species–area techniques, would be reduced by approximately 5 to 10%. These potential extinctions would not be immediate: it could take decades or even centuries to reach the new equilibrium number of species. Comparable estimates have not been made for the impact of habitat loss in other biomes.

For some groups of vertebrates and plants, between 5 and 20% of the identified species are already listed as being threatened with extinction in the foreseeable future. These estimates depend strongly on predictions of future rates of forest loss which may increase or decrease, and on the effects of fragmentation. They will also be modified by the effects of conservation action such as the protection of areas of high diversity.

Even if species do not become extinct, many of them will lose distinct populations or suffer severe loss of genetic variability through habitat loss or fragmentation. Natural and agricultural systems are being degraded through soil erosion, introduction of exotic species, fragmentation and pollution; the effects of these most recent human-induced changes will not emerge for some time yet – suggesting that a substantial increase in the level of future extinctions of species or populations as a result of human activity is already inevitable.

The underlying causes

The primary causes underlying the loss of biodiversity are demographic, economic, institutional, and technological factors, including:

- increasing demands for biological resources due to increasing population and economic development;
- failure of people to consider the long-term consequences of their actions, often due to a basic lack of knowledge;
- failure of people to appreciate the consequences of using inappropriate technology;
- failure of economic markets to recognize the true value of biodiversity;
- failure of economic markets to apply the global values of biodiversity at local level;
- institutional failure to regulate the use of biological resources resulting from the growth in urbanization, changes in property rights, and shifting cultural attitudes;
- failure of government policies to address the over-use of biological resources; and
- increasing human migration, travel, and international trade.

These underlying causes manifest themselves in the loss, fragmentation, and degradation of habitats; the conversion of natural habitats to other uses; overexploitation of wild resources; the introduction of non-native species; the pollution of soil, water, and atmosphere; and, more recently, signs of long-term climate change.

Without immediate action future options will be restricted

Unless actions are taken now to protect biodiversity, we will lose forever the opportunity of reaping its full potential benefit to humankind. Priority actions need to focus on improving the knowledge base, correcting past failures in policy and ensuring that conservation and sustainable use of the planet's resources and the equitable sharing of benefits are made an integral part of all socioeconomic development.

Managing biodiversity

The conservation and sustainable use of biodiversity needs to become an integral component of economic development by correcting policy and market failures. This will require much greater levels of co-operation and co-ordination than has previously been seen in traditional sectoral approaches to the management of natural resources. A balanced mix of incentives and disincentives, working alongside conservation laws, market adjustments, and traditional regulatory techniques, is needed in managing biodiversity at the national level. Institutional and legal frameworks are needed to ensure that conservation and sustainable use of natural resources are integrated successfully into the wide range of social, cultural and economic contexts in which actions must be taken.

The adoption of more ecologically based management systems, which take into account the effects on biodiversity of extracting goods and using ecological services promises a way of balancing human socioeconomic and long-term ecological considerations.

Conserving biodiversity

A wide variety of measures can be used to conserve biodiversity, including both in situ *and* ex situ *methods.* Effective *in situ* approaches include legal protection of endangered species, the preparation and implementation of species management or recovery plans, and the establishment of protected areas to conserve individual species and habitats. Protected areas generally must be augmented by additional measures, such as the preservation or establishment of safe corridors through areas of intensive human use, and must also return some economic benefit to local human populations if access and other restrictions are to be respected. Currently, the percentage of different biomes covered by protected areas ranges from less than 1% for temperate grasslands and lake ecosystems to nearly 10% for subtropical and temperate rain forests and islands.

Ex situ conservation centres such as arboreta, aquaria, botanic gardens, seed banks, clonal collections, microbial culture collections, field gene banks, forest nurseries, propagation units, tissue and cell cultures, zoological gardens, and museums, can help to conserve stocks of both wild and domesticated animals, plants, fungi and microorganisms, but are less able to maintain their populations. Serious gaps exist even in the *ex situ* coverage of those species that are known to be of direct economic importance, particularly in the tropics. Indeed the only species that have been sampled in any depth are some of the major crop plants, certain pathogens of humans and crops, and 'model organisms' used in scientific research.

Restoration and rehabilitation of habitats, which depend on the availability of material and its multiplication ex situ, *will come to play increasingly important roles in re-establishing degraded and damaged ecosystems.*

Sustainable use of biodiversity

Sustainable use of biodiversity is a key component of sustainable social and economic development. Management systems must take this into account explicitly, recognizing that social and economic measures may be just as important as technical considerations. Flexibility of management is needed so as to be able to respond to changing social, biological and physical environments, while still maintaining essential ecosystem functions. Appropriate incentives and the enforcement of management decisions and policies must be ensured. Finding the appropriate balance depends on the particular cultural, legal, economic, ownership, tenure and biological circumstances in each individual country.

Equitable sharing of benefits

An equitable sharing of income and assets is an important component of a strategy for conservation of biodiversity. In particular, an equitable distribution of the benefits of biodiversity conservation is a prerequisite for creating the incentives needed to maintain the Earth's biological wealth. Local benefit sharing has the effect of lowering the opportunity cost of forgoing conversion to commercial or other uses such as arable agriculture, pasture or industry.

The role of research, monitoring and inventory

Enhanced research, inventory and monitoring are important to promote responsible policy-making and management. Research into the uses and applications of biodiversity and its components is important as is further research into the ways in which biodiversity contributes to the provision of ecological services, so that those services can be sustained indefinitely. Monitoring and inventories are needed so that newly discovered life-forms can be properly documented and so that the status of individual species and particularly ecosystems can be gauged over time.

Building national capacity and expertise

Committed and skilled people are the key to successful maintenance and sustainable use of biodiversity. Training must be provided for those involved in managing protected areas, conducting biodiversity inventories, and developing and safeguarding *ex situ* collections of all kinds. An essential element in the training of the next generation of professionals will be the new focus on the broader aspects of resource management and the critical role of maintaining adequate levels of biodiversity in conjunction with the management of forestry, fisheries and agriculture. National training programmes and international exchange programmes must concentrate on producing more skilled scientists, particularly in the developing countries, and on improving the information-handling capacity of those countries through improved access to, and management of, information now available world-wide on computerized databases. Educating the public and making people aware of the issues involved in biodiversity are essential elements in improving the decision-making process.

Summary for Policy-Makers

Introduction

The Earth is home to a rich and diverse array of living organisms, whose species, the genetic diversity they comprise, and the ecosystems they constitute add up to what we call biodiversity (Box 1). Biodiversity is the natural biological capital of Earth. It provides the goods and services essential to human livelihoods and aspirations, and enables societies to adapt to changing needs and circumstances. For example, forested ecosystems provide fuels, medicines, construction materials and animal habitat; wetlands and riparian ecosystems protect water quality and aquatic life; oceans provide food and energy, and regulate climate, and agricultural systems produce food. Ecosystems also afford opportunities for recreation and tourism. More generally, ecosystems provide for the processing, storing and cycling of carbon and nutrients, thus influencing the Earth's climate and atmospheric composition.

Today, the scale of human impacts on the global biosphere is increasing dramatically due to activities that arise from the rapid growth in human population and increasing rates of consumption. Ecosystems are being altered and destroyed, while species in some groups of plants and animals are going extinct at rates some fifty to a hundred times higher than they otherwise would, and others are having their populations depleted. The genetic resources essential for industries such as agriculture, forestry and fisheries continue to be lost. This tragic loss and degradation of biodiversity holds serious economic, ethical and cultural consequences for humanity and the evolution of life on Earth. Indeed, the very foundation of sustainable development is being threatened.

Societies should consider carefully how they interact with biodiversity (Fig. 1). If responsible measures are taken now, losses or alterations can be slowed or in some instances halted by integrating biodiversity concerns into national decision-making processes using a combination of social and economic policies and incentives; by utilizing scientific and technical knowledge more effectively; by addressing the underlying causes of biodiversity loss; and by building human and institutional capacity world-wide.

One indication of the growing international concern about biodiversity was the emphasis given to the issue at the 1992 United Nations Conference on Environment and Development held in Rio de Janeiro and the ensuing Convention on Biological Diversity. The Convention recognizes that actions are needed to conserve biodiversity, ensure the sustainable use of its components, and ensure the fair and equitable distribution of the benefits derived from its use.

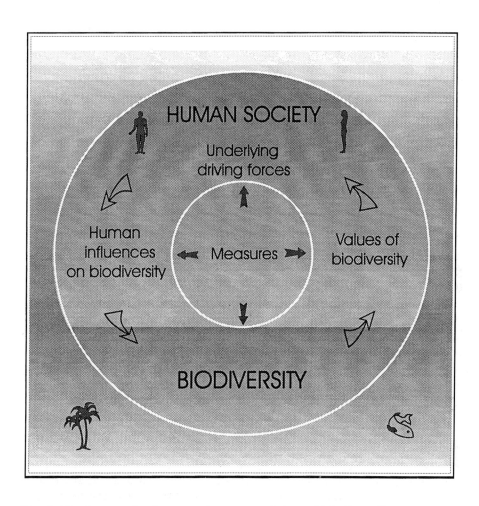

Fig. 1 The interaction between human society and biodiversity.

Box 1 What is biodiversity?

Biodiversity is defined by the Convention on Biological Diversity as *'the variability among living organisms from all sources, including terrestrial, marine and other aquatic ecosystems and the ecological complexes of which they are part; this includes diversity within species, between species and of ecosystems'*. More simply, biodiversity is the variety of the world's organisms, including their genetic makeup and the communities they form. Biodiversity is dynamic: the genetic composition of species changes over time in response to natural and human-induced selection pressures; the occurrence and relative abundance of species in ecological communities changes as a result of ecological and physical factors (Box 2).

Ecological diversity: Ecological systems do not exist as discrete units, but represent different parts of a natural continuum. Although terms such as forest, grassland, wetland and coral reef are commonly used to denote ecological systems, their delineation and spatial scale often depend on the intended purpose of the classification (Fig. 3).

Some commonly used terms are:

Biome – a continental-scale region characterized by its distinctive vegetation and climate

Ecosystem – the individuals, populations and species that occur in a defined area, including their interactions with each other and with their physical environment.

Ecological community – a group of species inhabiting a particular area.

Habitat – the biological and physical environment of a particular species.

Organismal diversity: The total number of species on Earth is estimated at between 13 and 14 million, of which only 1.75 million have been described. The enormous diversity between these species, ranging from common annual herbs to bacteria of deep ocean trenches, their arrangement into classifications reflecting their phyletic relationships, and the complex patterns of variation and distribution that they show, provide the very substance of biodiversity. Groups of interbreeding individuals within a species form distinct populations. Groups such as plants, birds, mammals, fishes, reptiles and amphibians – the species with which we are most familiar – account for only 3% of the estimated total, while the majority of species belong to groups such as insects, arachnids, fungi, nematodes and microorganisms (Fig. 2).

Genetic Diversity: Genetic differences between the individuals of a species provide the basis for the diversity that is found between species. Molecular studies have revealed a wealth of genetic variability in most species: in fact, individuals of virtually all species are genetically unique. Genetic diversity can be described at multiple levels from single genes to visible multi-locus traits. It is expressed as genetic variability both within and between populations. The amount and distribution of genetic diversity vary extensively among species in ways which are incompletely understood. It is well established, however, that genetic diversity within species is necessary to allow them to adapt to changing environmental conditions.

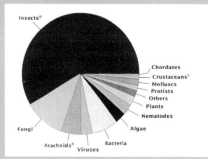

Fig. 2

1. * are arthropod groups
2. Chordates include mammals, birds, reptiles, fish and amphibia

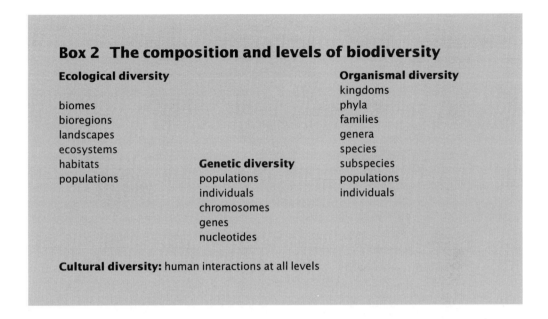

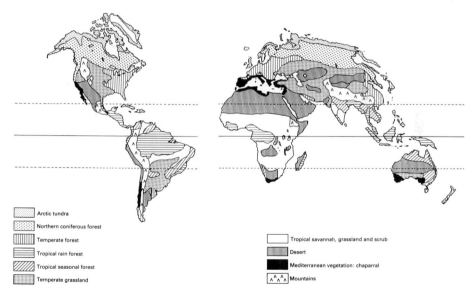

Fig. 3(*a*) Distribution of the world's terrestrial biomes (from Cox, C.B. and Moore, P.D. 1993. *Biogeography: An ecological and evolutionary approach.* Blackwell Scientific, London).

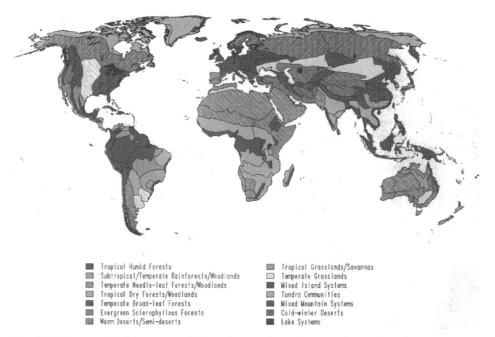

Tropical Humid Forests
Subtropical/Temperate Rainforests/Woodlands
Temperate Needle-leaf Forests/Woodlands
Tropical Dry Forests/Woodlands
Temperate Broad-leaf Forests
Evergreen Sclerophyllous Forests
Warm Deserts/Semi-deserts

Tropical Grasslands/Savannas
Temperate Grasslands
Mixed Island Systems
Tundra Communities
Mixed Mountain Systems
Cold-winter Deserts
Lake Systems

Fig. 3(*b*) The world's biogeographic realms and provinces (after Udvardy, M.D.F. 1975. *A classification of the biogeographical provinces of the world.* IUCN, Morges, Switzerland).

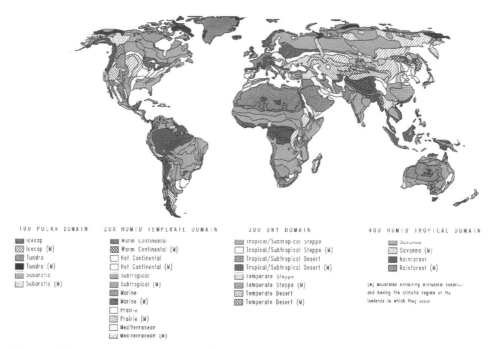

100 POLAR DOMAIN
Icecap
Icecap (M)
Tundra
Tundra (M)
Subarctic
Subarctic (M)

200 HUMID TEMPERATE DOMAIN
Warm Continental
Warm Continental (M)
Hot Continental
Hot Continental (M)
Subtropical
Subtropical (M)
Marine
Marine (M)
Prairie
Prairie (M)
Mediterranean
Mediterranean (M)

300 DRY DOMAIN
Tropical/Subtropical Steppe
Tropical/Subtropical Steppe (M)
Tropical/Subtropical Desert
Tropical/Subtropical Desert (M)
Temperate Steppe
Temperate Steppe (M)
Temperate Desert
Temperate Desert (M)

400 HUMID TROPICAL DOMAIN
Savanna
Savanna (M)
Rainforest
Rainforest (M)

(M) Mountains exhibiting altitudinal zonation
and having the climatic regime of the
lowlands in which they occur

Fig. 3(*c*) The world's ecoregions (after Bailey, R.G. and Hogg, H.C. 1986. A world ecoregions map for resource partitioning. *Environmental Conservation* **13**: 195–202).

The Global Biodiversity Assessment (GBA) is an independent, critical, peer-reviewed scientific analysis of the current issues, theories and views regarding the main aspects of biodiversity. It provides an analysis of a wide range of biological and social science issues related to biodiversity (Box 3).

Box 3 The Global Biodiversity Assessment

The GBA was endorsed by the Global Environmental Facility in 1992. A Preparatory Group was convened by the United Nations Environment Programme (UNEP) in March 1993 to develop objectives and a preliminary outline. In May 1993, UNEP approved the GBA project, and held the initial meeting of the GBA Steering Group to establish the policies for preparing the Assessment and to approve a draft list of contents. The major issues associated with biodiversity were addressed by establishing 13 Sections:

- Introduction
- Characterization of biodiversity
- Magnitude and distribution of biodiversity
- Generation, maintenance and loss of biodiversity
- Biodiversity and ecosystem function – basic principles
- Biodiversity and ecosystem function – biome analyses
- Inventory and monitoring of biodiversity
- The resource base for biodiversity assessments
- Data and information management and communication
- Biotechnology
- Human influences on biodiversity
- Economic values of biodiversity
- Measures for conservation of biodiversity and sustainable use of its components

Each Section was headed by a team of expert scientists, with up to four Coordinators and many Lead Authors chosen per Section in order to achieve broad geographical coverage and balanced representation of developing and developed country views. A total of over 400 experts from over 50 countries were formally involved. Teams met in one or more workshops to plan and write each Section. The draft text was submitted to extensive peer review: governments and organizations were asked to help nominate reviewers. More than 1100 scientific experts from over 80 nations were solicited for comments, resulting in more than 500 written reviews. The revised GBA Sections and a draft Summary for Policy-Makers (SPM) were then subjected to a comprehensive review workshop held in Panama in June 1995.

This SPM features those aspects of the full GBA that hold significant implications for Policy-Makers, including: the importance of biodiversity in human society; the distribution and magnitude of biodiversity; the influence of human activities on biodiversity; the consequences of changes in biodiversity; and the conservation of biodiversity, its sustainable use; and the fair and equitable sharing of benefits derived from its use. Although the SPM provides policy-relevant information, it does not make policy recommendations.

Biodiversity is essential to human well-being

Human societies rely on a vast array of biological resources and their diversity to provide for essential goods and services. *Direct uses* include the production of food, clothing, materials for shelter and fuel, and medicines. *Indirect uses* provide a wide variety of ecosystem services, such as the maintenance of the composition of the atmosphere, protection of watersheds and coastal zones, maintenance of soil fertility, and the dispersal, breakdown and recycling of wastes. In addition, *non-use* or *passive values* that are based on ethical, aesthetic, spiritual, cultural and religious considerations underlie many aspects of biodiversity's importance to humanity. In many cultures, these values are just as, if not more, important than those related to economic use. Indeed, most of the world's religions teach respect for the diversity of life and concern for its conservation. Examples of the various types of economic values that are assigned to biodiversity are listed in Box 4.

Indirect use values: maintaining the provision of goods and services

Ecosystems, such as agroecosystems, forests, rangelands and coral reefs, differ in their ability to provide goods and services, and improper management can reduce their ability to provide those goods and services. Where specific ecosystems provide essential services, such as wetlands for water purification and waste assimilation, it is important that the ecosystem be large enough in area for its ecological functions not to be significantly impaired. Consequently, poorly managed activities can lead to degradation. For example, the conversion of forests and other natural vegetation types has often led to soil erosion and stream sedimentation resulting in loss of soil productivity, aquatic life and flood protection. Similarly, large-scale habitat degradation in many arid and semi-arid regions has been shown to lead to increased desertification.

   Some species are known to be important for the proper functioning of an ecosystem but the roles served by most species are not understood. Indeed, some species have a significance out of proportion to their abundance, such as the regulation of plant uptake of soil phosphorus by species of mycorrhizal fungi. The loss of these 'keystone' species would greatly reduce the productive capacity of an ecosystem.

   The geographical position of an ecosystem and its spatial relationship with respect to other ecosystems of similar or different type is often an important consideration. For example, coral reefs, mangroves and kelp forests can buffer adjacent terrestrial systems from ocean waves, and thus mitigate the effects of storms that would otherwise produce substantial erosion (Fig. 4). Riparian areas and wetlands purify water before it reaches streams and rivers. Retaining appropriate vegetation in these areas is more efficient for maintaining this ecological service than retaining similar vegetation elsewhere. Likewise, many animals and birds need large habitat areas or corridors of habitat that link small habitat fragments. The degree of habitat fragmentation and connectivity can affect their ability to forage for food, locate cover, or reproduce successfully. For plants the spatial arrangement of ecosystems can affect seed and pollen dispersal and subsequent reproduction.

   The provision of goods and services sustainably over long periods of time requires the maintenance of biodiversity at characteristic levels to ensure their

Box 4 Economic perspectives of values assigned to biodiversity

Use values

Direct value: The value of those components of biodiversity that satisfy human society's needs.

Consumptive use of genes, species or ecological communities, or biological processes to meet needs, such as food, fuel, medicine, energy and wood. *Non-consumptive* use of components of biodiversity, such as recreation, tourism, science and education.

Indirect value: The value of biodiversity in supporting economic and other activities in society. This value stems from the role of biodiversity in maintaining ecosystem services that support biological productivity, regulate climate, maintain soil fertility and cleanse water and air.

Option value: The insurance premium people are willing to pay to keep the option of using biodiversity directly and indirectly in the future. The information or scientific option value of biodiversity is called quasi-option value.

Non-use or passive values

Non-use or passive values stem from altruism towards friends, relatives or other people who may be users (*vicarious use value*); altruism towards future generations of users (*bequest value*); and altruism towards non-human species or to nature in general (*existence value*). This may be motivated by moral, ethical, spiritual or religious considerations.

Vicarious use value: What people are willing to pay (or the benefits they are willing to forgo) to ensure that other members of the present generation enjoy access to specific components of biodiversity.

Bequest value: What people are willing to pay (or the benefits they are willing to forgo) to ensure that future generations enjoy access to specific components of biodiversity.

Existence value: What people are willing to pay (or the benefits they are willing to forgo) to ensure the continued existence of specific components of biodiversity. Existence value is sometimes referred to as intrinsic value.

continued ability to adapt to environmental and management perturbations. This is true of genetic diversity within species, species within ecosystems, and of ecosystems within a region. For example, because species often differ in their response to climate fluctuations, a change in climate may cause the local elimination of some species, while others will persist or may even flourish.

The direct use values of biodiversity

Of the estimated 240 000 known vascular plants, about 25% have edible properties. While 90% of human food supplied by only about 100 species, all communities in

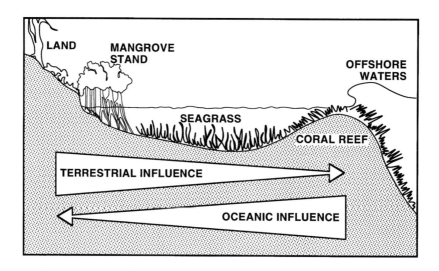

Fig. 4 The tropical coastal seascape showing buffering of the land from the ocean by reefs and the buffering of reefs from the land by coastal forests and seagrass beds (from Ogden, J.C. 1987. Cooperative coastal ecology at Caribbean marine laboratories. *Oceanus* **30**: 9–15)

fact depend on a much wider range of species as part of their daily lives. The centres of diversity for major crops are shown in Fig. 5. The ability to increase production of these food crops or to adapt commercial varieties to new pests and environmental conditions depends on the conservation, in gene banks, of the genetic diversity that has been collected by farmers over millennia as 'landraces' and that occurs in wild relatives. Recently, this has led to the breeding of greatly improved high-yielding rice and wheat varieties which have raised the value of annual crop yields in Asia by US$1.5 and $2.0 billion, respectively.

Marine fisheries provided about 84 million tonnes food for humans and live-stock supplements and earned US$11 billion dollars for developing countries in 1993. Artisanal fisheries currently provide approximately 25% of the global fish catch and about 40% of the fish used for human consumption and employ the vast majority of the world's fishers, especially in developing countries.

Advances in science, such as gene technology, are revealing new opportunities to generate economic and health benefits from biodiversity at the cellular and molecular levels. Biological processes are being used for industrial production and environmental clean-up; the health industry uses enzymes from a variety of organisms; new bioassay techniques render biochemical prospecting for new medicines and other products vastly more efficient and newly discovered interactions among species may themselves provide direct benefits (Box 5).

In 1993, about 80% of the 150 top prescription drugs used in the United States were synthetic compounds modelled on natural products, semi-synthetic compounds derived from natural products, or in a few cases natural products. In con-

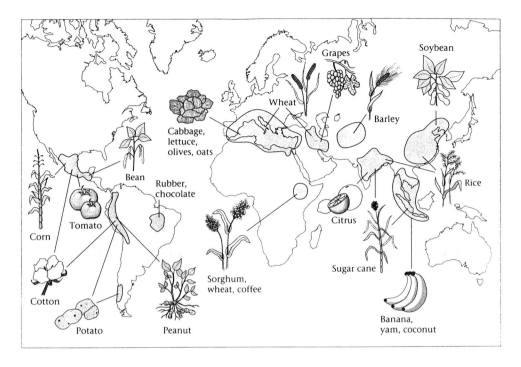

Fig. 5 The centres of genetic diversity for major crops (from Primack, R.B. 1993. *Essentials of Conservation Biology.* Sinauer Associates, Sunderland, Mass).

Box 5 An example of direct benefits from complex ecological interactions

The day-flying moth *Urania fulgens*, of northern South America and Mexico, provides an example of how complex interactions between species can provide ecological goods. The caterpillars of the moth feed exclusively on trees and vines of the genus *Omphalea.* When the caterpillar population reaches locally high levels the plants become heavily defoliated, and this heavy defoliation causes the trees and vines to produce protective chemical toxins. As the plants in a location become unpalatable the moths begin to migrate to new areas. In this case, the toxic plant compounds, which have been shown to be effective against the HIV virus *in vitro*, are produced only from the interaction between plant and moth and only when moth populations reach a threshold intensity.

trast, in China, for example, traditional drugs derived from medicinal plants accounted for about 40% of consumption of medicaments in recent years.

The World Bank estimates that activities related to tourism world-wide approach US$2 trillion annually. Ecotourism is emerging as one of the fastest-growing components of this industry, with as many as 235 million individuals participating in 1988, resulting in economic activity estimated at US$233 billion. More than half of this ecotourism was related to animals.

How much biodiversity is there and where is it found?

The distribution and magnitude of the biodiversity that exists today is a product of over 3.5 billion years of evolution, involving speciation, migration, extinction and, more recently, human influence. The current distribution and magnitude of biological diversity can be viewed at three levels: the diversity of ecological communities, species diversity, and genetic diversity.

Inadequate knowledge of the diversity of ecological communities

An ecosystem is a community of organisms and their environment which functions as an integrated unit. Forests are ecosystems. So are rotting logs, ponds, rivers, range-lands, whole mountain ranges, and indeed the planet itself. Ecosystems occur at many different scales, ranging from micro-sites to the biosphere, and species composition, structure and function within them changes continually over time. Ecosystems may grade into one another or be nested within a matrix of larger ecosystem units.

Ecosystems are frequently delineated along boundaries that correspond to variations in the physical environment – such as soil types, climate and elevation, and variation in faunal and floristic composition. Various classification systems have been devised, each of which defines bio-regions or ecosystems somewhat differently, but which also recognize many broad similarities (Fig. 3). Since ecosystems are often defined with a specific purpose in mind, there is no single measure of ecological community diversity which can be uniformly applied. In spite of the difficulty in classifying and delineating ecological communities, at large scales there is some sense of the distribution and extent of the various types of ecosystems, such as wet-lands or tropical forests.

The extent and distribution of species' diversity

Recent estimates of the total number of species range from 7 to 20 million, out of which we believe a good working estimate is about 13 to 14 million. Only about 1.75 million species have been described scientifically, of which slightly under a fifth are plants or vertebrates (Table 1; Fig. 6). Even for the 1.75 million species described there is no comprehensive listing. In many cases the area from which a species was officially described has been so dramatically altered that it is no longer possible to re-find the species there. Also, many of the earlier descriptions of species failed to record site characteristics and habitat conditions at the collection sites.

Estimates of species diversity are relatively good for plants and vertebrates although many remain to be described: in Brazil alone, five new species of monkey were described during the last decade. Less well characterized groups of organisms include bacteria, arthropods, fungi and nematodes, while species that reside on the

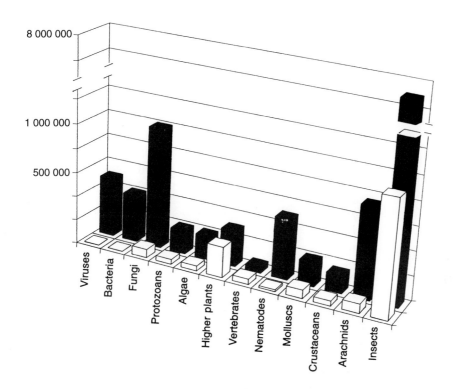

Fig. 6 Numbers of described species (open columns) and possibly existing species (dark columns) for those major groups of organisms expected to contain in excess of 100 000, with vertebrates for comparison (from Hammond, P.M. 1992. Species inventory. In: WCMC, *Global Biodiversity, Status of the Earth's Living Resources*, 17–39. Chapman and Hall, London).

deep-sea floor and below the ground are especially poorly known. Scientists know very little about most of the properties of most of the 1.75 million species that have been described, such as their reproductive biology, demography, the chemicals they contain, their ecological requirements and the roles they play in ecosystems.

Domesticated species represent a tiny fraction of Earth's biota. Of the estimated 320 000 vascular plant species, about 25% have edible properties, but only about 3000 species are regularly exploited for food. An additional 25 000–50 000 plant species are used in traditional medicine. Only about 30 of the estimated 50 000 vertebrate species have been domesticated. An additional 200 species of fish, molluscs, crustaceans, frogs, turtles and aquatic plants are grown for food and other products, and an increasing number of fungi and other microorganisms are also eaten or used in fermentation processes, in industrial processes, or for drugs. Additional efforts in taxonomy can aid in the identification of more economic uses (Box 6).

For many groups of terrestrial organisms the number of species tends to increase, and population size and range decrease, from the poles to the Equator.

Table 1 Approximate numbers of species in major groups.

The groups of organisms estimated to contain more than 100 000 species, with vertebrates and others listed for comparison (all numbers in 1000s).

Group	Number of described species[1]	Estimated total number of species in group
Viruses	4	400
Bacteria	4	1000
Fungi	72	1500
'Protozoa'[B]	40	200
'Algae'[B]	40	400
Plants	270	320
Nematodes	25	400
Crustaceans	40	150
Arachnids	75	750
Insects	950	8000
Molluscs	c. 70	200
Vertebrates	45	50
Others[3]	115	250
Totals	1750	13 620

Note: 1. Estimated number of described species that are accepted today.
  2. The Protozoa and Algae are interpreted here in a broad sense.
  3. Mainly little-known animal groups.

However, there are numerous exceptions, and there are many groups of organisms for which we lack information on which to base informed statements. In the oceans, the variation in numbers of species follows a less defined pattern. Marine organisms tend to be more widely distributed due to the absence of physical barriers; they travel large distances, often with the aid of ocean currents, and those organisms that are rooted or stationary have easily dispersed seeds or larvae.

Endemic species or relict species are those that are naturally restricted by geographic features, such as mountains, islands, peninsulas, continents or other physical features, or where unique local conditions (such as serpentine soils) lead to the evolution of species suited only to that specific environment. Remote oceanic islands have the world's highest percentages of endemic species, with only a small proportion of their native species being found anywhere else. In some situations 'relict' species represent the last remaining populations of formerly much more widely distributed species.

Inadequate knowledge of the genetic variability within species

Each species contains an enormous quantity of genetic information, and there is often substantial diversity in the genetic make-up of populations within a species.

Box 6 Biological classification – an essential tool for recognizing and understanding biodiversity

Discovering, describing and classifying species and their genetic variation allows us to 'take stock' of biodiversity, handle it and communicate about it, and describe and analyse the patterns that it forms. Classifications of organisms into species, genera, families, orders, classes, phyla, and ultimately the five generally recognized kingdoms of animals, bacteria, fungi, plants and protoctists, are based on their systematic and evolutionary relationships. These classifications are highly predictive and provide a framework that serves both as a reference tool and a summary of evolutionary relationships. For example, these relationships can be used to identify species with potentially similar uses. The chemical taxol, a valuable anti-cancer drug, was originally discovered in a small population of North American yew (*Taxus brevifolia*). Scientists were able to predict its probable occurrence in other species of the genus and were thus able to extract a precursor to taxol on a sustainable commercial scale from the commonly occurring European yew (*Taxus baccata*). Frequently, taxonomic information is used to trace the geographical origins of agricultural pests and diseases, thereby leading to the identification of potential biological control agents. Taxonomic insights can also be important for conservation management strategies. For example, it is important to consider whether a species of concern is the sole survivor of an evolutionary line, or is closely related to many others.

Depending on the details of the species' breeding system, the variability within populations may be as great as, or greater than, the variability between populations. However, with few exceptions we have only rudimentary knowledge of the products or functioning of most genes.

Domestication for agriculture has led to the development of many cultivated crop varieties and livestock breeds. The number of distinct samples of germplasm collected for major crops ranges from 50 000 to 125 000 for maize, rice, barley and wheat. Although some genetic diversity has been lost as traditional breeds or varieties have been replaced by modern high-yielding disease-resistant forms, enormous genetic diversity is still seen in the large numbers of varieties grown in local regions. For example, Andean farmers cultivate thousands of different clones of potatoes, more than 1000 of which have different names, while in Europe, more than 700 unique breeds of cattle, sheep, pigs and horses have been identified.

Human demands and failures in economic markets: the underlying drivers of change

The rate at which humans are altering the environment, the extent of that alteration, and the consequences of these changes for biological diversity are unprecedented in human history, and are now beginning to pose substantial threats to the economic and cultural life of many societies. Depending on the circumstances, human activities may increase, maintain, or diminish the diversity of species, genes or ecological communities in a given region and at a given time, but the general trend is an increasing loss of biodiversity at the global scale. Some of these changes, such as extinction of species, are truly irreversible; others are not, but the challenge of managing natural resources without losing biodiversity has increased markedly. The transformations people have already made in land use have created conditions for extinctions that will persist for centuries, even if further destruction or degradation of habitats were halted immediately. Moreover, pressures on biological diversity are likely to increase still further as a consequence of human-induced climate change.

The underlying causes of the loss and degradation of biodiversity are:

- increasing demands for biological resources stimulated by population and economic development;
- failure of people to consider the long-term consequences of their actions, often due to a basic lack of knowledge;
- failure of people to appreciate the consequences of using inappropriate technology;
- failure of economic markets to recognize the true value of biodiversity (Box 7);
- failure of economic markets to apply the global values of biodiversity at local level;
- institutional failures to regulate the use of biological resources as a consequence of changes in human values related to the urbanization of societies, institutions, property rights and cultural attitudes;
- failure of government policies to correct for the resultant overuse of biological resources; and
- increased human migrations, travel, and international trade.

The specific mechanisms by which the underlying causal factors result in the reduction and loss of populations, the extinction of species and the transformation and degradation of ecological communities include:

- habitat loss, fragmentation and degradation (or the transformation of ecological communities to other uses);
- over-exploitation;
- the introduction of non-native species;
- pollution or toxification of the soil, water and atmosphere; and
- climate change.

In continental terrestrial ecosystems, the most important mechanism is the loss, fragmentation and degradation of habitat. On islands, species introductions and habitat loss have been equally important mechanisms. In oceans, overharvesting and pollution are the most important factors. All of these mechanisms have been major influences on species and populations in freshwater ecosystems.

The speed and scale of changes in biodiversity

The impact of human activities on ecosystems

The net effect of human activities may possibly be a greater overall diversity in the types of ecosystems and landscapes around the world, some of which are extremely important to societal well-being. Human activities are directly responsible for creating agroecosystems and cultural landscapes, for example. However, these increases in the diversity of ecological systems have come at the expense of

Box 7 Economic markets and policies do not reflect the full value of biodiversity

The economic challenge in managing biodiversity is to balance the benefits derived from exploitation of individual biological resources against the true social costs caused by the loss of the diversity of organisms and ecological communities. The private profit to be gained from transforming a habitat or over-exploiting a species may be substantial to an individual, but it is often less than the true cost to society. This is because the markets which determine the private profitability of using biological resources often ignore the wider costs of that use. They generally fail to capture the indirect use value of biodiversity in supporting a range of ecosystem services including, for example, water purification, regulation of runoff, waste assimilation, habitat provision and carbon storage. Furthermore, economic markets generally fail to accurately reflect the ethical, cultural, aesthetic and religious value of biodiversity. Because many of the costs of biodiversity are external to the market, they are ignored by private decision-makers. This often leads to the overuse or misuse of biological resources through such actions as deforestation or excessive harvesting of species. The challenge for policy-makers is to design institutions and incentives that will:

- confront resource users with the full social cost of their behaviour;
- adjust the current distortions in economic markets; and
- enable those who invest in maintaining biodiversity to reap the benefits.

Policies to achieve these goals must be formulated in a wide variety of sectors that have not traditionally examined their consequences for biodiversity: e.g. agriculture, forestry, fisheries, energy and transportation.

impoverishment of a great number of natural communities, and the reduction of at least some ecosystem services.

Although total area may or may not have changed for major vegetation types, the plant species composition within them has often been dramatically altered by practices such as various forms of logging, grazing, introduction of exotics and fragmentation, to the extent that many ecosystems contain only one or a few plant species, and at times no longer include any of the original species. For example, many native grasslands no longer exist as such, their species composition having been altered by the introduction of cattle and sheep. Northern temperate forests have changed dramatically in North America and Europe as a consequence of intensive logging, exploitation, and replanting, often with introduced species, over the last several hundred years. In terms of total area, forest and woodland communities have decreased globally by about 15% since pre-agricultural times. Northern temperate forests are currently relatively stable in total area. In the early to mid-1980s, humid tropical forests were losing approximately 10 million hectares, or just under 1% per year globally, although there is good evidence that rates of forest conversion in parts of Central and South America have declined since. Dry tropical forests may have lost even more area. Since 1700 there has been a five-fold increase in cropland, and since 1800 about a 24-fold increase in irrigated crop land (Table 2). The total area of grassland has remained roughly constant over the past 300 years, with loss through conversion to cropland being balanced by gain through deforestation.

Coastal and lowland areas, wetlands, native grasslands and many types of forests and woodlands have been particularly influenced or destroyed. For example, the dry tropical forest of the Pacific coast of central America once covered 550 000 square kilometres; now, less than 2% is intact. The United States has lost 54% of its wetlands; Thailand has lost more than 50% of its mangroves, and the Atlantic forest of Brazil has been reduced to approximately 10% of its original 1 million square kilometres. Of a total area of 600 000 square kilometres of coral reefs, about 10% have already been eroded beyond recovery.

Loss of populations and species

Human impacts tend to severely reduce the size of many biological populations (Fig. 7), greatly increasing the risk that populations will be lost locally, and ultimately leading to some species' extinction. The loss of genetically distinct populations within a species is almost as important as the loss of an entire species. Population Viability Analyses for vertebrates and plants show that in some cases when numbers of individuals in a population decline to as low as a few thousand, random variation in environmental factors can rapidly lead to total extinction. Even when the species does not go extinct, its loss from a local region or a major reduction in its population can have significant consequences for human livelihoods and ecological services.

Mass extinctions of biodiversity have been recorded in the geological record (Fig. 8). It has been suggested by some authors that we are on the verge of a further mass extinction spasm. During the past few thousand years human activities have

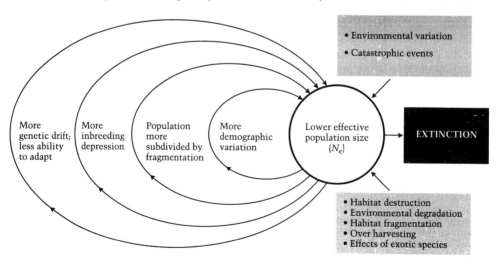

Fig. 7 Human impacts tend to severely reduce the size of many biological populations, greatly increasing the risk that populations will be lost locally, and ultimately leading to some species' extinction (source as Fig. 5).

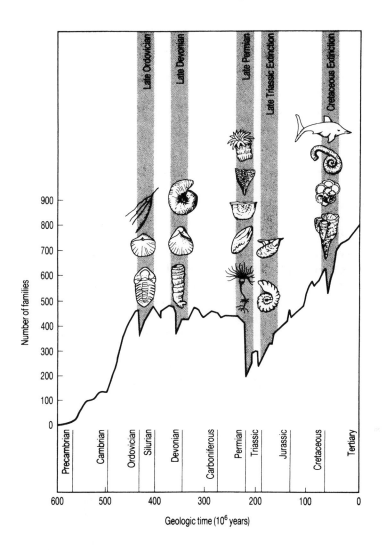

Fig. 8 A summary of mass extinctions showing the principal groups of animals affected by each event (from Given, D. 1992. *Principles and Practice of Plant Conservation*. Timber Press, Oregon).

led to the extinction of species. The prehistoric colonization of the Pacific and Indian oceans by humans and their commensals such as rats, dogs and pigs, may have led to the extinction of as many as a quarter of the world's bird species. Since the year 1600, 484 animal and 654 plant species (mostly vertebrates and flowering plants) are recorded as having gone extinct, although this is certainly an under-recording, especially as regards the tropics. The rate of recorded extinctions in well-known groups such as birds and mammals has increased dramatically during this period: 38 species between 1600 and 1810 compared to 112 species between 1810 and 1992 (Fig. 9). Extinctions during these 390 years have been most numerous on islands and island archipelagos, and in freshwater ecosystems. Evidence suggests that extinction rates are lower in floras and faunas that have already undergone some form of severe environmental stress. For example, recent extinction rates in Mediterranean floras are much lower (0.1%) in the Mediterranean proper where human impacts are oldest, than in Western Australia (1%), where human impacts are more recent.

Among organisms with adequate fossil records, including invertebrates, mammals and diatoms, the average 'life-span' of a species has been calculated to be of the order of 5–10 million years. If this were to be applied to our estimate of approximately 13.5 million species of all groups currently alive, this would suggest that the expected current rates of extinction would be roughly one to three species per year. There is, however, uncertainty about the average 'life-span' of species in the fossil record and there is variation in life-span estimates for different groups of organisms. Mammals have a relatively short average species 'life-span' of about 1 million years, suggesting that one extinction would be expected approximately every two centuries, on average. The uncertainty as to the total number of extinctions among vertebrates and plants over the past century makes it impossible to assign a single estimate to recent extinction rates, but at least among vertebrates and vascular plants the recent rates are fifty to a hundred times the expected background.

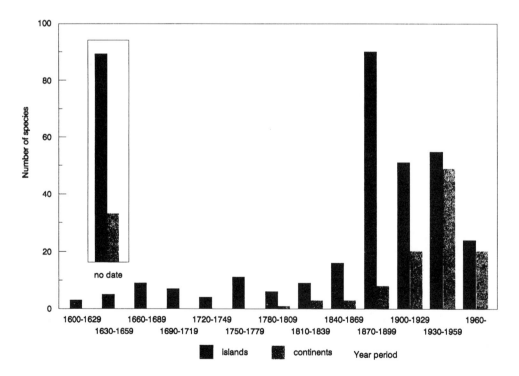

Fig. 9 Time series of animal extinctions on islands and continents: all taxa (from WCMC *Global Biodiversity, Status of the Earth's Living Resources.* Chapman and Hall, London).

Table 2 Global human-induced conversions in selected forms of land cover.

Cover	Date	Area ($\times 10^6$ km²)	Date	Area ($\times 10^6$ km²)	Percentage change
Cropland	1700	2.7	1990	14.4	+530
Irrigated cropland	1800	0.1	1989	2.0	+2000
Closed forest	pre-agricultural	46.3	1983	39.3	−15
Forest and woodland	pre-agricultural	61.5	1983	52.4	−15
Grassland/pasture	1700	68.6	1980	67.9	−1

Two quantitative methods have been used to estimate pending rates of extinction. The first uses careful demographic analyses in selected species, and one assessment has projected that 50% of species in selected subsets of mammals, birds and reptiles are likely to go extinct within 100 to 1000 years. Because of the stringent requirements for data, this approach has only been applied to a small number of very well known species. The second approach uses the observation that the total number of species found in an area is related to the size of that area in a fairly simple way, quantified by a species–area curve. Several estimates have been made of the potential loss of species due to tropical deforestation by using this empirical relationship and making assumptions about the future rate of loss of habitat. Published estimates of species that will become extinct or committed to extinction in tropical forests over approximately the next quarter-century range from 2% to 25% in the groups examined (variously: plants, birds, birds and plants, and all species). This would be equivalent to 1000 to 10 000 times the expected background rate. If recent rates of loss of closed tropical forest (about 1% globally per year) were to continue for the next 30 years, the equilibrium number of species in the forest, as calculated by species–area techniques, would be reduced by approximately 5 to 10%. These potential extinctions would not be immediate: it could take decades or even centuries to reach the new equilibrium number of species. Estimates are likely to be most accurate for groups such as beetles, birds, plants and mammals, for which empirical data are easily available, but they may apply equally well to less-studied groups. These estimates do not take into account the potential effects of fragmentation, increases or reductions in the rate of deforestation, or the potential effects of mitigative measures that might be taken in the interim that could retard or even prevent extinctions, such as the setting aside of protected areas which include 'hotspots' or concentrations of species' diversity. Comparable estimates have not been made for the potential impact of habitat loss in other regions.

More qualitative methods of assessing the probability of species' long-term survival use the categories of IUCN – The World Conservation Union. Threatened species are those that are thought to be at significant risk of extinction in the foreseeable future because of random or deterministic environmental factors, or by virtue of their rarity. Estimates for regions are constructed by taking into account those species for which enough is known about their population size, trends, and potential threats, and extrapolating estimates of habitat loss. In 1994, the minimum estimate for numbers of globally threatened animal and plant species was about 5400 animals and 26 000 plants (Table 3). About 11% of bird species, 18% of mammals, 5% of fish, and 11% of plants were catalogued as threatened. An analysis of the change in species' categorizations over time implies that 50% of bird and mammal species will be extinct within 200–300 years although these changes in status reflect not only biological factors but the state of knowledge of the species involved and the rate of data entry. However, for the vast majority of the 1.75 million described species or the many millions of undescribed species, no assessment of status has been made.

Genetic diversity is being eroded

Many samples of crop varieties and livestock that have been displaced by the worldwide spread of new varieties are now conserved *ex situ* (off site) in seed banks, field gene banks, and through cryopreservation of semen and embryos, or *in situ* on-farm conservation programmes. For example, plant germplasm collections hold approximately 4 million samples, representing at least 10 000 species in total. About 3 million of those accessions relate to only about 100 species. However, losses of genetic resources still continue in *ex situ* collections, due to lack of resources for appropriate management, such as the need to germinate seeds periodically in order to maintain the viability of the collection, and in some cases whole collections are at risk or have even been lost. There are very few samples of wild species in gene banks. It is important to recognize that *ex situ* collections no longer continue to evolve in response to new environmental conditions: only wild populations continue to do so, and thus only wild populations can provide a continually evolving suite of genes from which to draw. Loss of cultural information about how to use the varieties in *ex situ* collections is also quite serious.

Table 3 Number of species considered 'Threatened' by the World Conservation Monitoring Centre (WCMC classifies all species listed as 'Endangered', 'Vulnerable', 'Rare' or 'Indeterminate' as threatened species). (WCMC pers. comm. 1995.)

Threatened	Endangered	Vulnerable	Rare	Indeterminate	Total
Mammals	177	199	89	68	533
Birds	188	241	257	176	862
Reptiles	47	88	79	43	257
Amphibians	32	32	55	14	133
Fishes	158	226	246	304	934
Invertebrates	582	702	422	941	2 647
Plants	3 632	5 687	11 485	5 302	26 106

For most wild species, little information is available on the extent of the loss of genetically distinct populations and consequent genetic erosion (Box 8). Each one of these populations may house genes, gene combinations or adaptations which are unique. Species that are already threatened probably suffer from some loss of genetic diversity because of population loss, while the genetic composition of some wild populations of species has also been altered by genes from introduced species. Reduction in population size normally increases the rate of loss of genetic diversity and can lead to substantial reductions in adaptational fitness, especially in cross-breeding species.

Ecological consequences of reductions in biodiversity

The consequences of different ways of losing biodiversity for the sustainable provision of goods and services are described here.

Transformation and fragmentation of communities

Some fragmentation of existing ecological communities is inevitable, except in areas that have been specifically protected. In nearly all cases, the fragmentation reduces the diversity of native species in their natural habitats. The species most likely to be lost are large predators and other species with large body sizes and large area requirements. Also likely to be lost are species less able to disperse and colonize habitat patches. Species likely to survive fragmentation will be those best adapted to patchy and frequently disturbed environments, such as early successional and easily dispersed species. Fragmentation is thus expected to result in ecosystems dominated by opportunistic species, i.e. those characterized by good dispersal and colonizing abilities, rapid growth and short life cycles. Such systems have characteristically higher losses of nutrients, nitrogen and carbon; higher litter quality and therefore faster decomposition rates; simpler spatial structure; and less overall protection from herbivores than the original communities that preceded them.

Box 8 Loss of genetic diversity in salmonids

Loss of genetic diversity at multiple levels in wild species can be exemplified by salmonid fishes. These fishes are typically structured genetically and the occurrence of local adaptations is well documented. In some salmonids, hundreds of local populations have been extirpated or are threatened because of pollution, dam-building and other forms of water use. Loss of genetic diversity within populations has occurred in several species following hatchery programmes which were based on few parental fish. In addition, genetic diversity between populations has been compromised by both the intentional and accidental release of non-native (including cultured) populations into environments inhabited by wild populations of the same species. Thus genetic erosion occurs both within and between several salmonid species and some releases have even led to the introgression of genes from one salmonid species into the gene pool of another.

The transformation, fragmentation and loss of habitats has had many different effects on the provision of ecological goods and services. The massive creation of new agroecosystems has increased food production dramatically. At the same time, it has led to the impoverishment of natural communities and can reduce the ability of ecosystems to maintain productivity in the face of environmental fluctuation. Substantial alteration in soil fertility can be driven by changes in plant species composition and microbial groups required for the cycling of important plant nutrients. The loss of particular plant species and loss of critical communities, such as forested watersheds, can reduce the ability of some ecosystems to control soil erosion and retain water. Conversion from forest or shrubland to grassland dramatically increases stream flow, and if this occurs in the upper reaches of a watershed, it can increase the need for additional water control measures through dams and other measures to combat increased flooding and sedimentation.

Increases in the extent and yield of rice agroecosystems have provided food for vast numbers of people, especially in Asia. At the same time, these increases in rice cultivation and numbers of livestock have been major contributors to the increased methane concentrations in the atmosphere, and thus to concerns over greenhouse warming. It is likely, although less certain, that increases in the use of nitrogenous fertilizer in the tropics are also contributing to rising concentrations of nitrous oxide, a very powerful greenhouse gas. Large-scale transformations of habitat can also affect the local climate. Deforestation has also led to major malaria outbreaks in the western Amazon, due to the creation of new habitats for mosquito vectors, and to increased colonization by susceptible human populations.

The large-scale transformation of forested ecosystems to pasture, grassland and agriculture has been an important contributor to the increase in atmospheric carbon dioxide over the last several hundred years. The first phase of this transformation occurred in the developed countries of the north, but in recent decades, tropical conversion of forest to grassland has become the main contributor. During the 1980s, conversion of tropical forest contributed approximately 1.6 gigatonnes of carbon per year to the atmosphere, in addition to the 5.5 gigatonnes released by fossil fuel combustion. This was slightly offset by regrowth of temperate and boreal forests, which sequestered about 0.5 gigatonnes per year during the same time period. Improved management of forested ecosystems and reforestation in both temperate and tropical regions can continue to sequester carbon from the atmosphere and move it to longer-lived soil pools, thus reducing the rate at which greenhouse gases are added to the atmosphere.

Within reasonable bounds, we cannot consider transformations of ecological communities to have only local effects. In marine systems, changes in geographically distant ecosystems may greatly affect one another through, for example, larval transport or the transport of pollutants by currents. In terrestrial ecosystems, changes in one area may have atmospheric consequences that affect other regions, while loss of habitat may affect species that range widely, thus affecting other distant ecosystems. Fragmentation of temperate forests in North America can, for example, affect the survival of tropical–temperate migratory birds, which are important seed dispersal and biological control agents in neotropical areas. The transformation of forested ecosystems affects atmospheric composition on a global scale.

On a less dramatic scale, changes in forested watersheds can affect water flow and quality far downstream.

Overexploitation of resources

Overexploitation of resources, such as poorly managed cropping and timber harvesting, while providing food and wood also tends to disrupt ecosystem services by decreasing the ability of the ecosystem to retain nutrients, water and topsoil. These effects are due directly to the process of extracting the desired materials, along with the longer-term biogeochemical effects of removing carbon, nitrogen and nutrients. Over the long term, reductions in soil carbon and soil fertility, and increases in overland flow and sedimentation rates are often the result. Increased fertilizer and pesticide subsidies are then often required to maintain adequate agricultural yields, resulting in increased direct costs.

The period from 1950 to 1970 saw the collapse of many of the world's largest fisheries for small pelagic species, primarily through overexploitation. All but one (Icelandic spring-spawning herring) have recovered, though to varying degrees and at various rates. More recently, many of the major fisheries in the North Atlantic have collapsed through overfishing.

Invasions and introductions

International travel and trade have provided many opportunities for the deliberate introduction or accidental invasion of species (Box 9). When a species enters an ecosystem in which it previously did not occur, it can adversely disrupt ecosystem processes, or – less commonly – have positive effects such as biocontrol of pests or

Box 9 Introductions of genetically modified organisms

Introduced species or varieties, whether developed through traditional breeding methods or through genetic engineering, have the potential to affect both ecological relationships and evolution. Genetic material from introduced plants, animals and microorganisms can be transferred into wild populations of related species through the formation of fertile hybrids. The new genetic material can then potentially alter the ecological interactions of that wild relative. For example, a disease or frost resistance gene transferred into a wild weedy relative of the crop could extend the range of that wild relative. In aquatic systems, substantial gene flow occurs between hatchery-reared fish and wild populations. To date, in agricultural systems, most gene flow has taken place between crops and their weedy relatives.

Once a species is released or a new gene is introduced into a population, there is usually no means of undoing that action. Using current methods for modelling eco-systems, we cannot reliably predict the outcome of the release of new species or new cultivated varieties. Effects of new genes or new species on population dynamics are extremely sensitive to environmental influences and their manifestations are often slow to be recognized.

pathogens in an agroecosystem. Introductions of agricultural species into new regions, beyond the range of their natural predators and pathogens, have often resulted in increased yields and improved economic returns. However, introductions of exotic species in many freshwater ecosystems for sport or food have led to loss of native species (Fig. 10), and subsequent alterations in many ecosystem processes. Microbial species introductions, particularly of plant pathogens, have had a large effect on ecosystem composition in both natural and managed systems, but these effects do not always have large observable effects on ecosystem processes. For example, the loss of chestnut from the eastern deciduous forests in North America, due to the introduction of chestnut blight from Europe, was both rapid and dramatic, but there have been no discernible consequences for ecosystem functioning, as

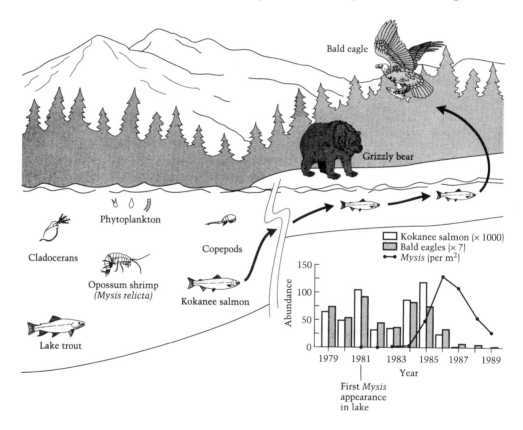

Fig. 10 In the flathead lake and its tributaries in Montana, the food web was disrupted by the introduction of the opossum shrimp (*Mysis relicta*). The natural food chain involved grizzly bear, bald eagles, and lake trout eating kokanee salmon; kokanee eating zooplankton (cladocerans and copepods); and zooplankton eating phytoplankton (algae). Opossum shrimp, introduced as a food source for the salmon, ate so much zooplankton that there was far *less* food available for the fish. Kokanee salmon numbers than declined radically, as did the eagle population that relied on the salmon (source as Fig. 5).

other tree species seem to have fulfilled the chestnut's original functional roles. On the other hand, introductions of pests and pathogens into agricultural systems typically pose great danger of loss of productivity and yield. Introductions of new capabilities, such as nitrogen fixation, into ecosystems whose component species previously did not have this ability, typically have dramatic effects on both composition and ecosystem functioning. The introduction of nitrogen-fixing trees into sites in Hawaii has led to a complete restructuring of the plant communities, with consequent increases in nutrient supply and fire frequency, leading to rapid losses in the populations of the original species. Systems with limited genetic diversity, especially crops, are often the most susceptible to the effects of introductions and invasions, with the introduction of pathogens being of primary concern.

Islands and ecosystems with relatively few component species, such as boreal forests, seem to be more susceptible to species introductions than species-rich biomes such as tropical forests, so it would be expected that establishment of introduced species leading to disruption of ecosystem processes is more likely to occur in the former than in the latter. Freshwater ecosystems in all climatic zones also seem to be especially sensitive to invasions and introductions. In general, areas that have been subjected to disturbance or stress from other environmental factors, such as fire, drought, overgrazing or extensive clearing, can provide open habitat and resources for introduced species to exploit. Whether or not the introduced species will spread depends on the particulars of their biology, and the biology of the native species they encounter. The combination of introduction of non-native species and overexploitation of resources has been especially prevalent in grassland ecosystems. On the one hand this has stimulated ranching activities that have been economically productive. On the other hand, in arid and semi-arid regions, the introduction of cattle, sheep and other non-native grazers, if poorly managed, can result in invasion by new plant communities, soil compaction and desertification.

Apart from these generalizations, there is very little ability to predict *a priori* the effects of accidental or deliberate introductions, suggesting that considerable prudence should be exercised.

Pollution of soil, water and atmosphere

Pollutants stress ecosystems and may reduce populations of sensitive species. For example, acid deposition (sulphate and nitrate) has made thousands of lakes virtually lifeless in Scandanavia and North America and, in combination with other kinds of air pollution (e.g. ozone), has damaged forests throughout Europe. Acidic deposition has also been implicated in other effects, e.g. trace element deficiencies in the diet of moose, leading to increased mortality, and birds producing eggs with thin and porous shells, resulting in a high incidence of clutch desertion and empty nests. In addition, air pollution has been linked to the impoverishment of grasslands in Poland where plant diversity and growth have been severely reduced and soil fauna decreased. Marine pollution, particularly from non-point sources, has severely affected the Mediterranean and many coral reefs, estuaries and coastal seas throughout the world, thus impacting the reproduction of some marine species.

Long-term climate change

In the coming decades anthropogenic climate change, otherwise known as global warming, could adversely affect the world's living organisms, especially when coupled with population growth and accelerating rates of resource use. The Earth's climate is projected to warm by 1–4 °C during the next 100 years, alter precipitation patterns and lead to an increase in sea level of 10–120 cm. These projected changes in climate would cause a poleward migration of certain species by hundreds of kilometres and an altitudinal displacement by hundreds of metres. Many species will not be able to redistribute themselves fast enough to keep pace with the projected changes in climate. Considerable alterations in ecosystem structure and function are likely, with some loss of species. Figure 11 illustrates some natural and human impediments to the poleward migration for temperate forest species. Flora and fauna in coastal ecosystems and on small islands will be adversely affected by projected increases in sea level. Because carbon dioxide is the dominant greenhouse gas directly affected by human activities its beneficial affects on productivity need to be considered.

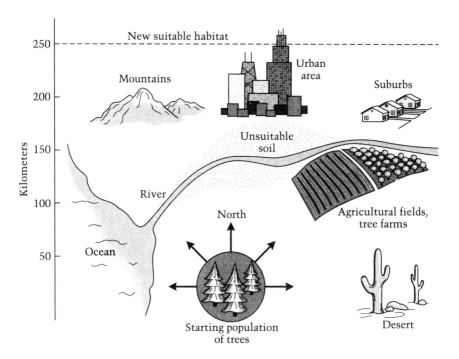

Fig. 11 If global climate increases over the next century as some models suggest, north-temperate tree species will have to disperse 160–640km (From: Intergovernmental Panel on Climate Change, 1995) northward in order to find sites with a hospitable climate. Not only will these species encounter natural barriers such as mountains, oceans, rivers, and unsuitable terrain, but they face barriers created by people such as agricultural fields, cities, suburbs, roads and fences (source as Fig. 5).

Loss of ability to resist or recover from disturbance

Reductions in species diversity can lower an ecosystem's ability to resist stress from other environmental factors, and to recover from disturbance. Experimental studies have shown that species-rich temperate grasslands exhibit smaller changes in plant biomass after drought than is the case in less rich areas. The existence of relatively undisturbed communities within a mosaic of different land uses can serve as sources of propagules, seeds and dispersing animals to recolonize areas that have been adversely affected by other stresses.

The sensitivity of ecosystems to changes in biodiversity appears to be influenced in part by the number of species that influence individual ecosystem processes in similar ways. For example, the ecosystem-level consequences of species losses should be greatest for systems that have few species, such as boreal forests, deserts and islands, because there will be few species that can substitute for the missing taxa, and thus the chance of even a single loss adversely affecting an ecosystem process is high. In addition, since each individual species may play many different functional roles, ecosystems with few species may lose important functions by the deletion of even a single species. Conversely, ecosystems with many functionally similar species should be better protected from disruptions, because there are more species available to react to the environmental stress. On short time scales, some degree of substitutability can be documented, as shown by experiments in a grassland system, when dominant species fully compensated for the removal of subordinate species while the subordinate species only partially compensated for the removal of dominant species. The variety of functional roles that individual species play in ecosystems is seldom fully known. Indeed, it is known that some species have functional roles that seem to be far out of proportion to their abundance. There is no *a priori* means of predicting which species will exhibit this characteristic, leading to inherent limitations in our ability to predict the results of losing particular species. Modern agriculture and plantation forestry are based on the premise that low-diversity ecosystems can be highly productive. While this premise is broadly validated in intensively managed ecosystems, the experience of agriculture highlights the critical sensitivity of low-diversity ecosystems to variation in climate as well as outbreaks of pests and pathogens.

When changes in ecosystem composition and functioning do occur, they are often gradual. However, some ecosystems exhibit dynamic thresholds in their response to a major stress or disturbance – notably islands, lakes and agroecosystems. Others, such as boreal, Arctic and alpine systems, seem susceptible to chronic stress. No biome remains unaffected by landscape-scale changes in diversity, particularly those changes due to anthropogenic alterations. The large-scale conversion of ecosystems within landscapes tends to have long-lasting effects on system processes irrespective of whether the particular ecosystems were originally of high or low diversity. The efforts of human-induced change on biodiversity and on the functioning of ecosystems, together with the feedbacks involved, are conceptualized in Fig. 12.

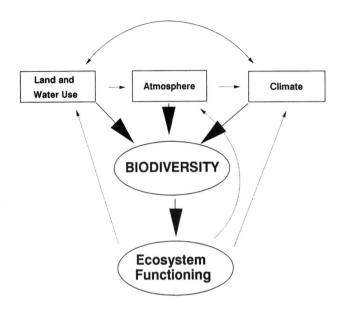

Fig. 12 Conceptual model of the effect of human-induced changes on biodiversity and on the functioning of ecosystems, together with the feedbacks involved.

Conservation, sustainable use and equitable sharing of benefits

The objectives of conserving biodiversity, ensuring its sustainable use, and ensuring the equitable sharing of benefits form the foundation of the Convention on Biological Diversity.

> The mutually reinforcing objectives of the Convention
> on Biological Diversity

The three issues of conservation, sustainable use and equitable sharing of benefits from biodiversity are not separable. Effective national action depends on developing an institutional and legal framework that integrates the benefits gained from conservation and sustainable use of biodiversity into national decision-making. It is important to recognize the social, cultural and economic contexts in which actions are contemplated, including the importance of local knowledge and values. Experience shows that the most successful regional and national strategies integrate all these factors (Fig. 13).

Economic and institutional factors play important roles in integrating the objectives of the Biodiversity Convention. Biodiversity management calls for greater levels of co-operation and co-ordination than are found in traditional sectoral approaches and while certain management activities, such as setting up protected areas or gene banks, may be targeted explicitly at biodiversity, most effects on biodiversity result from the secondary consequence of activities such as agriculture, forestry, fisheries, water supply, transportation, urban development, energy and so forth. Management objectives must incorporate the concerns and aspirations of the

Levels For Action

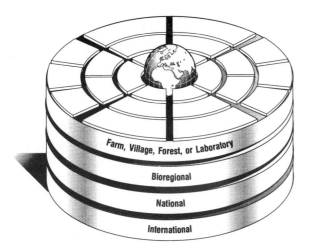

Fig. 13 The three issues of conservation, sustainable use and equitable sharing of benefits from biodiversity are not separate. Experience shows that the most success-ful regional and national strategies recognize the social, cultural and economic con-texts of biodiversity, including the importance of local knowledge and values (from WRI/IUCN/UNEP, 1992. *Global Biodiversity Strategy: Guidelines for Action to Save, Study and Use Earth's Biotic Wealth Sustainably and Equitably.* World Resources Institute, Washington DC, IUCN – The World Conservation Union, Gland, Switzerland, and the United Nations Environment Programme, Nairobi, Kenya).

many stake-holders, including local communities. Objectives must also be identified at a geographic scale large enough to allow flexibility in implementation in order to adapt to changing conditions, ensure the protection of critical habitat, and maintain the ecosystem processes that provide goods and services. Often, management actions are taken on scales that are too small to have the desired effect, or they fail to incorporate the many small individual resource management decisions, each with minimal impact on its own, but which together have significant impacts on a regional scale.

Increasing our understanding of biodiversity's benefits, and the ways in which our perception of these change over time, is a critical task. Experience with mechanisms for benefit-sharing is very recent, and not yet well understood. Most experience to date has come from agreements that regulate access to genetic resources by private companies, and from experimenting with different ways of appropriating the benefits to national and local beneficiaries, thus treating international and national aspects simultaneously (Box 10). Another important concern, however, is the degree to which knowledge and understanding of biodiversity is gained and shared. The role of research and monitoring is especially critical, since these activities underlie countries' abilities to take advantage of the cultural and economic opportunities afforded by biodiversity, and to make informed decisions about its ultimate uses.

Technology can be an important tool for managing biodiversity well. Agricultural technology, for example, has often led to major increases in food production when used appropriately. New technologies, such as low-impact agriculture, have the potential to maintain or even further increase yields, while reducing unintended adverse environmental impacts. The advance of biotechnology (Box 11) holds promise for increasing the benefits of biodiversity, while at the same time introducing additional concerns over unintended consequences

Equitable sharing of benefits

Poverty and an inequitable distribution of income and assets is both a cause and a consequence of biodiversity loss. The poorest individuals and societies often face the largest relative effects from biodiversity loss, and the lowest incentives to conserve biodiversity. An equitable distribution of income and assets is an important component of a strategy to conserve biodiversity. In particular, an equitable distribution of the benefits of biodiversity conservation is a prerequisite for creating the incentives needed to maintain the Earth's biological wealth.

In many cases an equitable sharing of benefits requires local benefit sharing. This is particularly important for conservation projects or for integrated conservation and development projects.

Local benefit sharing has the effect of lowering the opportunity cost of forgoing conversion to commercial alternative uses, such as arable agriculture, pasture or industry (Box 12).

Wide-ranging approaches to conservation

Conservation measures require both *in situ* and *ex situ* methods (Fig. 14). Effective *in situ* approaches for the conservation of individual species include legal protection of

Box 10 Economic tools and incentives

Economic and financial policies that could help address local market failures by capturing for local populations the benefits from goods and services derived from biodiversity conservation include:

Lowering forest protection costs. Costs can be reduced by directly involving the local populations in the protection and management of natural ecosystems (as guards, tour guides, collectors of non-timber forest products and scientific samples).

Using water fees as ecosystem conservation incentives. Local communities derive little benefit from maintaining watersheds, since the principal beneficiaries are located downstream. Water and hydropower pricing that includes a watershed protection charge levied upon farmers and urban and industrial users provides a way of compensating local communities.

Internalizing ecotourism benefits. The portion of ecotourism benefits that flow to the local population can be expanded by engaging local people as guards and tour guides, and by issuing ecotourism franchises to communities and allocating a portion of the ensuing revenues to the development of local employment opportunities.

Reforestation incentives. Land owners who keep their land in forests can receive a tax credit. Since this approach is especially beneficial to large, wealthy owner a system can be devised whereby small-holders can earn tax credits that they can sell to wealthy taxpayers having high taxes to offset.

Differential land use taxes. Categories for classifying land uses can range from environmentally most beneficial (e.g. natural forest) to environmentally most destructive (e.g. industrial site). To internalize the environmental cost of habitat conversion, a charge is imposed on land owners when land use is changed from a higher to a lower class.

Environmental performance bonds. Environmental bonds shift responsibility for controlling deforestation, monitoring and enforcement to individual producers and consumers who are charged in advance for the potential damage. These bonds can ensure that adequate measures are taken to minimize environmental damage and that funds are available for restoration of environments if compliance is poor.

Forest compacts. Compacts are undertaken by one country with the support of another to engage in policy reforms, conservation, and investment programmes that achieve specified targets of sustainable forest management or preservation in exchange for financial and technology resources. For example, Carbon Offsets agreements have been established between a power utility company in a developed country and a developing country to finance a shift to more sustainable logging practices in exchange for tax credit by the utility for the carbon stored or retained on sites by the funded forestry activity.

Transferable development rights (TDRs) and conservation easements. These policy instruments enable a country or private land owner to sell the 'right' to convert a natural habitat for a price that fully covers the opportunity cost.

Box 11 Opportunity and concerns raised by biotechnology

Biotechnology can provide important advances in the use of genetic and biological resources for economic gain. It provides a means of using living organisms to produce important chemicals for medicine and industry; it can be harnessed for environmental remediation; and it provides enzymatic reactions used in industrial processes. Biotechnology also provides tools for advancing our understanding of the living world, and thus may aid the assessment and monitoring of biodiversity. It can contribute greatly to biodiversity conservation *in situ* and *ex situ*, thereby enhancing our ability to manage biodiversity wisely.

The Convention on Biological Diversity calls for measures to ensure the safe transfer, handling and use of modified organisms resulting from biotechnology. Because of the potential for great benefits from biotechnology, its use is increasing rapidly, and thus questions about its safety have been raised. The direct impacts of biotechnology can be ecological or evolutionary, operating through biological processes, e.g. gene transfer to non-target populations. Many countries have already devised scientific methodologies for assessing the probability of negative impacts through field and laboratory trials. Although negative impacts cannot be completely ruled out, these methods provide a way of evaluating the risks involved, and therefore should allow maximum benefits to be gained from biotechnology applications.

endangered species, the preparation and implementation of management or recovery plans, and the establishment of protected areas specifically to protect particular species or to protect unique genetic resources such as wild relatives of crop species. Large protected areas have the advantage of protecting large numbers of species at the same time, but can be justified in their own right for their protection of the diversity of different ecological communities, letting natural processes continue to operate, and thus preserving the natural communities' ability to provide ecosystem services. The proportion of biomes covered by protected areas ranges from less than 1% for temperate grasslands and lake ecosystems to nearly 10% for subtropical and temperate rain forests and island ecosystems. Table 4 shows the distribution of protected areas by biome type, while Table 5 shows the percentage of African countries' bird species found within protected areas. Countries vary considerably in the proportion and degree to which their land areas are protected.

The effectiveness of conservation actions varies dramatically, and the management of protected areas around the world faces serious obstacles. The establishment of areas in which all economic activity is restricted may conflict with the needs of local people, so that park boundaries and regulations are not observed. Many designated protected areas are not effectively managed due to a lack of trained personnel, financial resources or ecological knowledge and as a consequence face serious threats from agricultural expansion, resource extraction, tourism and poaching. Protected areas generally must be seen in the context of overall landscapes and augmented by additional measures, including the preservation of natural corridors

Box 12 Local sharing of the non-use values of biodiversity

Since many of the social values ascribed to biodiversity are 'non-market' values, a large discrepancy persists between the private and social values accorded to it. In general, global markets are lacking for many of the values that people place on biodiversity or with the environmental benefits associated with it: for example, carbon storage in forests, or the existence values placed by people in the North on biodiversity of the South. The lack of such global markets means that these values cannot be appropriated by the people of the South. Furthermore, many existing economic incentives (i.e. subsidies) promote over-harvesting and depletion. For example, some countries consider land not used for agriculture as 'unproductive' and tax it at higher rates than agricultural lands.

Private and social values can be brought into better alignment by altering the incentive structure to favour conservation and sustainable management. This involves raising the local benefits from diverse ecosystems and lowering the opportunity costs of forgoing the conversion of natural ecosystems to alternatives such as agriculture, pasture or settlement. Local economic benefits from biodiversity can be enhanced by:

- establishing a secure set of property or use rights;
- insuring access to credit, markets, technology and education;
- providing mechanisms that fully value biodiversity and transfer part of this value to the local population; and
- involving local communities in the protection and management of the resource.

More generally, changes in the behaviour and management practices of local people can be encouraged through the use of:

- direct incentives, such as tax breaks, subsidies, grants, compensation for animal damage, interest-free loans, differential fees and differential access to resources;
- indirect incentives, such as the application of fiscal, service, social and natural resource policies to specific conservation problems;
- disincentives, such as penalties, punishment and other forms of law enforcement accompanied by public information.

within a matrix of more intensive human uses, and must return some economic benefit to local populations in order to succeed.

Ex situ conservation centres – arboreta, aquaria, botanic gardens, seed banks, clonal collections, microbial culture collections, field gene banks, forest nurseries, propagation units, tissue and cell cultures, zoological gardens and museums – can all help to conserve stocks of both wild and domesticated animals, plants, fungi and microorganisms, but are less able to maintain populations.

While *ex situ* facilities can provide genetic material needed for breeding programmes to improve and maintain domestic plants and animals, serious gaps exist in the coverage of those species that are of known, direct economic importance, particularly in the tropics. Exceptions include major crop plants, certain pathogens of humans and crops, and 'model organisms' used in scientific research. Most *ex situ*

Ex Situ Conservation

In Situ Conservation

Field Genebanks

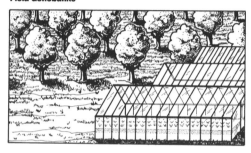

Fig. 14 Conservation measures require both *in situ* and *ex situ* methods (source as Fig. 13).

facilities – notably botanic gardens, zoological gardens and aquaria – also heighten public awareness of biodiversity and provide material for basic and applied scientific research in such areas as reproductive biology, genetics and systematics. Figure 15 shows the inverse relationship between the global distribution of plant species and botanic gardens. All *ex situ* facilities are potentially vulnerable to pests and diseases, physical damage from fires and floods and economic or policy changes.

Reintroduction of species and restoration and rehabilitation of habitats will come to play increasingly important roles in re-establishing biological diversity. They depend on both *ex situ* and *in situ* approaches. No menu of methods for sustainable use of biodiversity can ever be completely successful, and we are already faced with the prospect of needing to return ecosystems damaged by unsustainable practices to a state where ecological goods and services can be restored to acceptable levels. Methodologies for restoration are showing rapid advances, though technical and ecological challenges still hinder efforts to restore some species, communities and ecosystem services. Setting priorities for restoration and rehabilitation is a major challenge, particularly when these activities may require ongoing subsidies to maintain goods and services at acceptable levels.

Sustainable use of biodiversity

Sustainable use of biodiversity is considered today to be a prerequisite for sustainable social and economic development. Properly done, it ensures the continuing pro-

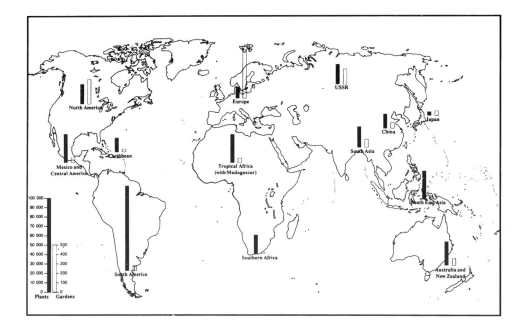

Fig. 15 World distribution of plant species and botanic gardens (from WWF and IUCN-BGCS, *Botanic Gardens Conservation Strategy*. IUCN, Gland).

vision of goods and services from ecosystems and their components. In order to use biodiversity sustainably, it is essential to have a basic understanding of ecosystems, their components, and the social and economic pressures that affect them. Resource management practices that use our knowledge of the processes in intact ecosystems are often more effective and less costly than those that do not. For example, forestry practices that mimic the frequencies of natural disturbances such as fires, appear to offer the best opportunities for maintaining the biodiversity associated with many forest ecosystems. In fisheries, better monitoring of fish stocks offers hope for increasing the sustainability of harvests and the conservation of marine biodiversity.

Social and economic measures may be more important than technical measures for ensuring sustainable use. For example, the assignment or recognition of clearly defined property rights and tenure systems is vital to sustainable forestry and fisheries. Of particular concern are equitable measures to transform open access regimes to private, community or other ownership systems to bring to a halt the overexploitation of forest, freshwater and marine ecosystems.

Many traditional resource management systems achieve effective conservation of biodiversity and sustainable use of its components. Small-scale farmers using traditional agricultural practices have long created varietal diversity and been stewards of genetic diversity (Fig. 16). Traditional forms of agriculture, particularly in developing countries, are the largest repositories of crop and livestock genetic diversity. On-farm conservation of crop genetic resources in traditional agroecosystems pro-

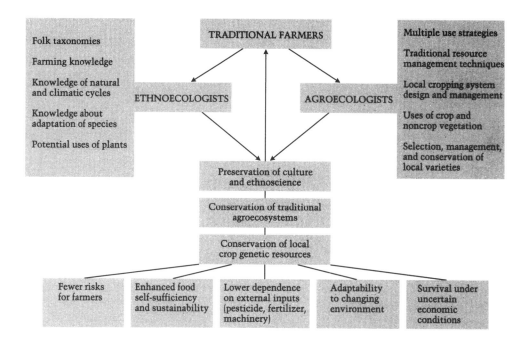

Fig. 16 Many traditional resource management system achieve effective conservation of biodiversity and sustainable use of its components (from Primack, R.B. 1993. *Essentials of Conservation Biology.* Sinauer Associates, Sunderland, Massachusetts, USA).

vides unique benefits due to the potential for continued, dynamic adaptation of plants to the environment, especially in diversified agricultural areas where crops may be enriched by gene exchange with wild or 'weedy' relatives in fields or adjacent ecosystems. These resources can be lost, however, in regions where conversion to high-input, low-diversity agroecosystems is economically more advantageous. Market mechanisms or funds that compensate farmers for providing this 'service' could in principle reduce the loss of these resources.

Tourism and other non-consumptive uses of biodiversity can provide opportunities for sustainable use, and can also be combined with other uses, such as bio-prospecting, so as to generate multiple income streams from single areas or resources. The success of such management schemes often depends on appropriating some of the benefits for the local communities.

Appropriate incentives and enforcement of management decisions and policies must be ensured. For example, an appropriate balance between national and local control over resource management is vital to sustainable use of biodiversity in providing goods and services of direct economic benefit. Over-centralizing resource rights has often led to excessive resource harvesting and biodiversity loss. Conversely, similar destructive practices have also resulted from too much local control over resources, particularly among communities without a long traditional attachment to a region or among communities that are confronted by rapid change due to population growth, expanding market forces and cultural breakdown. Finding the appropriate balance depends on the particular cultural, legal, economic, ownership, tenure and biological situations within countries. Wherever the balance lies in a particular case, incentives should be put in place to encourage adoption of the declared management policies, and enforcement of reasonable policies must be clear.

No management prescriptions can possibly anticipate all the possible changes in ecological, climatic, social and economic conditions. Hence, flexible techniques are needed for managers to maintain the provision of goods and services and respond to changing social, biological and physical environments, while reducing uncertainty about the functioning of ecosystems and therefore the effectiveness of their actions. *Adaptive management* is an emerging philosophy for integrating these concerns. It has three primary elements:

- management interventions are purposely made in an experimental manner so that the outcome of the intervention can be used to reduce uncertainty about the system;
- sufficient monitoring prior to and during the intervention enables detection of the results of the management intervention and thereby allows managers to learn from past experience; and
- based on the feedback to managers, communities and other constituencies, management interventions are then refined.

Importance of research, monitoring and dissemination of information

Enhanced scientific research and monitoring are essential for countries to increase their ability to benefit from and sustainably manage their biodiversity and its components. Particular areas for research and monitoring include:

- exploration, inventory and taxonomic studies to discover new organisms and understand the characteristics of related organisms and the patterns of variation that they make;
- ecological studies to understand the processes that sustain the provision of goods and ecosystem services; and
- monitoring programmes (Box 13) to determine the changing status of biodiversity and its components, thereby enabling appropriate management actions to be taken when needed.

A considerable amount of information on biodiversity does exist, but is difficult to gain access to, not always because of technological problems, but also because of differing policies on data ownership and control, and institutional rivalries. These policies must be analysed, and if necessary altered in such a way that benefits derived from the use of information help defray costs of providing information services. The rapid developments in information technology have provided new options for information access, use and management. Better software tools in local languages will facilitate the strengthening and decentralization of management systems and provide better support to decision-makers. The increased development of networks is opening new ways of accessing and exchanging information at national and global levels, and the emergence of new tools such as electronic publishing and multimedia will further facilitate the delivery of information. Careful analysis of technological options will help reduce the technology gap between countries and develop more efficient approaches to information management. Figure 17 illustrates how information needs to flow among different users.

Box 13 Monitoring biodiversity

Biological monitoring programmes can evaluate the trends in the status of species, communities and ecological systems over time. The conservation of biodiversity can be enhanced by monitoring programmes, providing a 'feed-back loop' that signals to managers and policy-makers the need to make appropriate changes. Monitoring programmes should be designed at a scale relevant to the ecological processes being monitored and the pertinent conservation or management questions being asked. Often, regional- or landscape-scale monitoring is necessary to evaluate the aggregate impact on species or ecosystems of local activities or events. Similarly, both a national and a global scale are needed to understand and effectively manage such species as migratory birds. Monitoring programmes need to be evaluated over time to refine techniques and to test new technologies.

Remote sensing from satellites and aircraft can be used to monitor changes in the extent of land cover, the distribution of major vegetation types, and the functioning of some types of ecosystems (Fig. 18). It can be used to stratify ecological sampling and to identify situations where more detailed, ground-based monitoring is warranted. Carefully chosen, indicator species provide an efficient means for monitoring the status and trends in the populations of some other species and certain ecosystem services. However, no small subset of indicator species can be used to monitor all aspects of biodiversity relevant to management.

Building national capacity and public awareness

Human, institutional, financial and infrastructure components are often scarce in much of the world, but can be expanded with well-focused investment and policy support. In many countries the existing telecommunications infrastructure is inadequate for the dissemination of information through electronic networks, and its improvement is an urgent priority.

Committed and skilled people are the key to the successful maintenance and sustainable use of biodiversity. Training for the people who will manage protected areas, conduct biodiversity inventories and develop and safeguard *ex situ* collections must be provided through appropriate mechanisms. Of equal importance is to re-orientate the training of the next generation of professionals who will manage biological resources such as forests, fisheries and agricultural lands in order to emphasize the benefits of maintaining adequate levels of biodiversity. Because of the continued importance of scientific research and monitoring, it will be particularly important to have trained scientists in all countries. The current distribution of expertise is strongly skewed towards the northern industrialized countries. Training and exchange programmes should therefore concentrate on producing more skilled scientists in the developing world, and providing them with the necessary research and management tools.

Important though scientific research and monitoring is, it is not sufficient by itself. The successful implementation of strategies to use biodiversity sustainably is

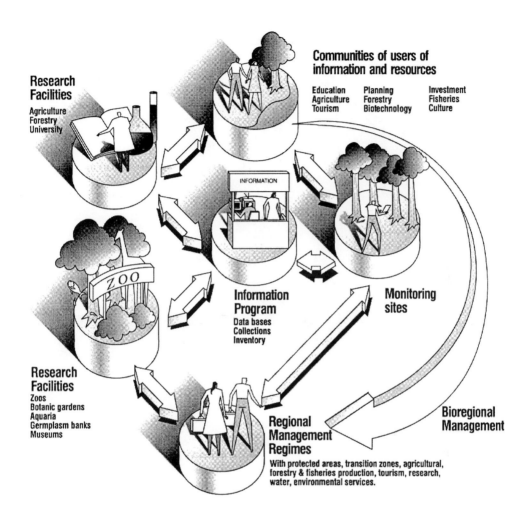

Research Facilities
Agriculture
Forestry
University

Communities of users of information and resources

Education	Planning	Investment
Agriculture	Forestry	Fisheries
Tourism	Biotechnology	Culture

INFORMATION

ZOO

Information Program
Data bases
Collections
Inventory

Monitoring sites

Research Facilities
Zoos
Botanic gardens
Aquaria
Germplasm banks
Museums

Regional Management Regimes
With protected areas, transition zones, agricultural, forestry & fisheries production, tourism, research, water, environmental services.

Bioregional Management

Fig. 17 Information flow on Biodiversity (from WRI/IUCN/UNEP, 1992. *Global Biodiversity Strategy: Guidelines for Action to Save, Study and Use Earth's Biotic Wealth Sustainably and Equitably.* World Resources Institute, Washington DC, The World Conservation Union, Gland, Switzerland, and the United Nations Environment Programme, Nairobi, Kenya).

often constrained by lack of public understanding and support. Broad constituencies of informed people need to be built up, and local and national experience and knowledge will play a critical role in developing well-informed citizenries. Governments themselves need to become better informed about biodiversity so that they will be able to make more informed decisions concerning the management of their natural resources.

NDVI May 1987

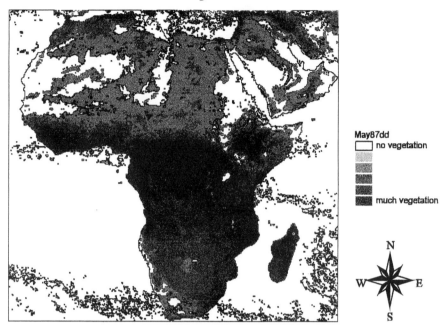

NDVI May 1986

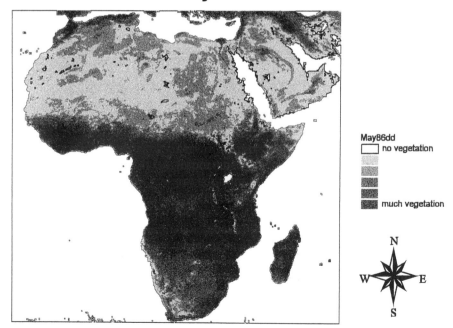

Fig. 18 Remote sensing can be used to monitor changes in the vegetation (UNEP/GRID).